Scrapbooking For Kids

(ages 1 to 100)

by Jill Haglund

SCRAPBOOKING FOR KIDS
BY JILL HAGLUND
1st Edition

ISBN 1-891 898-01-9, Library of Congress , Catalog Card Number 98-96811

This book was produced by TweetyJill Publications, Inc.
5824 Bee Ridge Road, Suite 412, Sarasota, Florida 34233, 1-800-595-5497

GRAPHIC DESIGN AND LAYOUT	Carol King
EDITOR	Kerry Arquette
COPY EDITOR	Deborah Mock
PHOTOGRAPHY CREDITS	Herb Booth, Booth Studio, Inc.
	Michael Heintz, Heintz Wasson Photography, Inc.
	Christopher Darling Photography
PHOTO STYLIST	Dale Clancy
	Rachel North
ILLUSTRATOR	Kristine Boshell
SCRAPBOOK ARTISTS	Jill Haglund
	Lori Pieper
	Sharon Kropp
	Norma Manak

NOTICE OF LIABILITY

TRADEMARKS

COPYRIGHTS

Note: All patterned papers featured are archival and by The Paper Patch Company® .
Family Treasures® punched shape is Swirl punch used on page 82.
Clearsnap® Top Boss™ Embossing Pad is used on page 85.
Elmers® Craft Bond™ Acid-Free Glue Stick is used throughout the publication.
Pebbles In My Pocket® Tracers™ featured on pages 61, 72, 86, 93, 104, 105, 111, 116.

First Edition - February, 1998
Second Edition - January, 2002

Printed in the United States of America by Quebecor world, Central Florida Press Orlando, Florida

THANK YOU

TweetyJill Publications would like to extend a heartfelt thanks to the many who were involved with this book— for their support, their encouragement, and for the giving of their time and talents.

Thank you to Booth Studio, the patient photo stylists, all the kids involved in the photography: Lindsay, Matthew, Joel, Sarah, Mariela, Michael, Aaron, Susan, Milan, Alan, Anthony, Olan, Althia, Ashley, Cinthia, Bryan and especially to the cover kids, Jason and Megan.

A special thank you for the gifted talents of Lori Pieper, Sharon Kropp and Norma Manak, the scrapbook artists; and our wonderful graphic designer, Carol King, who touched the book and made it just what we wanted.

Doing the publication was a fun experience and may not have become a reality without the encouragement from these special individuals: Karen Wiessner, Gordon Haglund, Marilyn Haglund, Cynthia Byers, Jeanne Reed of the International Scrapbook Trade Association, Cynthia Bricking, C.J. Wilson, and Sandi Griffith.

We want to express genuine appreciation to all the manufacturers involved:

Mix 'n Mats, Templates and Edgers, Doodads, Viewlers and Designer Letters by The C-Thru® Ruler Company.

Paper, Adhesive, Shapes, Photo Corners and Albums by CANSON®

Archival Quality, Acid-Free Markers, Pens and Glues by ZIG Memory System®

Acid-free stickers by Stickopotamus®

The Journaling Genie by Chatterbox Publications®

Die Cut System and Die Cut Shapes by Accu/Cut®

Acid-Free Storage Boxes, Adhesive, Albums, and Photo Marking Pen by EXPOSURES®

Cropper Hopper Scrapbook Tote, Supply Case, and Photo Case by Cropper Hopper

Albums by (bound + d/termined)®

Alphabet Stencils are Tracers® by pebbles in my Pocket®®

Portable Paper Trimmer, Circle Cutter, Stacker Stamps, Ink Pad, Paper Edgers, and Corner Edgers by FISKARS®

Punches, Corner Rounder, Nuetral 7 Acid-Free Tester Pen, Flash-Out Red-Eye Eliminator and Embossing Heat Tool by MARVY UCHIDA

Other books by TweetyJill Publications:

Scrapbooking As A Learning Tool
*Educators supplement to Scrapbooking
for Kids (ages 1-100)*
A wonderful resource for teachers and parents wanting to
incorporate scrapbook projects into an educational curriculum.
Projects include: My Autobiography, ABC-it's All About Me,
Character Building, Portfolios, plus others.

The Idea Book for Scrapbooking
An absolute must for all scrapbook enthusiasts! This one-of-a-
kind idea book has over 500 beautiful and unique page layouts.
Diverse styles and assorted techniques make this book an
excellent source for ideas and inspiration. We've complies and
published this collection of memory book pages by some of the
finest scrapbook designers in the country. Organized by
themes for easy reference. This is one book you'll use and love.

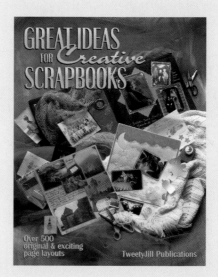

The Complete Guide To Scrapbooking
Snap! Your camera just captured a precious moment. Preserve it and
all the other smiles, tears, celebrations and life milestones within a
scrapbook that will keep them safe for generations. Over a million
women across America have discovered the fun and fulfillment of
scrapbooking. Now it's your turn! The Complete Guide To
Scrapbooking will introduce you to products, tools and techniques
you'll need to turn album pages into works of art. There are also
dozens of great project ideas to keep you inspired for years to come.

To order 1-800-595-5497
or see our website www.tweetyjills.com

A NOTE FROM ME TO YOU

Do you remember being born? Your huge, long-lashed eyes took in the world for the first time, and you were curious about everything.

Do you remember your first haircut? Your locks fell like rose petals, and your mom got all teary because her baby was growing up too fast.

Do you remember the first time you tried to ride a bicycle? It was more exciting than scary, and even when you fell and bruised your knees, you got up and tried again because you couldn't wait to "ride fast" with your friends.

Do you remember?

Probably not, because memories are slippery things. They have a funny habit of sliding out of reach just when we tell ourselves, "I'll never forget." That's sad, because memories are our souvenirs of where we've been and what we've done. So, keeping memories alive is important and lots of fun!

Scrapbookers are experts at keeping memories alive. They take photographs and mementos (cards, tickets, brochures, etc.) and combine them with written information to create personal "memory" albums. These albums can include lots of stuff or just a few special chosen items. They can tell the story of a single event such as a birthday or a week at summer camp, or they can tell about things that happen over several years. It is up to you, the artist.

The scrapbook you start today will be something you enjoy tomorrow. So, dive into the wonderful world of scrapbooking and before you know it you'll be cropping, matting, journaling and designing like a pro!

I know you can do it...I believe in you...have fun!

TABLE OF

1 WHAT IS CREATIVE SCRAPBOOKING?   I

    Safe   5

    Meaningful   7

    Creative   11

2 GETTING ORGANIZED   18

    Gather, Sort and Label Photos   20

    Storage   24

3 PUTTING THE PIECES TOGETHER   26

    Cropping   28

    Cropping With A Trimmer   29

    Silhouette Cropping   31

    Cropping With Templates   32

    Cropping With Mix 'n Mats   36

    Matting   38

    Double Matting   39

    Paper Edgers (or Decorative Scissors)   43

    Corner Edgers   44

    Corner Rounders   46

    Mounting Your Photos   48

    Pocket Pages   50

4 LETTER PERFECT   52

    Lettering Ideas   56

    The Journaling Genie   62

    Journaling With Templates   63

CONTENTS

What you're gonna find inside

5 DIE CUTS 64

Die Cut Tips and Tricks 66

Punches Are Just Mini Die Cuts 70

6 BORDERS 72

Rulers (with pens, paper and punches) 74

Doodads 79

Paper and Ruler Borders 80

7 FINISHING TOUCHES 82

Rubber Stamps 84

Embossing with Rubber Stamps 85

Paper Embossing 87

Circle Cutter 88

8 PROJECTS AND PAGES 90

All My Adorable Pets 92

Cookin' Up Somethin' Special 94

Collector's Album 95

Be A Sport 96

Personal History Album 98

Teen Memories 100

School Days 102

Car Trip Keepsake 103

Birthday Bash Book 106

Cousins By The Dozens 108

Grandparent's Gift 110

Adventurous Vacations 114

Camp and Camping Fun 116

SCRAPBOOKING IS SAFE, MEANINGFUL, CREATIVE. SCRAPBOOKING IS

CHAPTER 1

WHAT IS

CREATIVE

SCRAPBOOKING?

INTRODUCING

JASON

Woof! In dog talk that means, "Hi guys. I'm man's best scrapbooking friend!" (We dogs don't waste words.) I'm going to help lead you down the album-making path. So, shake a tail and follow me! I'll tell you why scrapbooking is safe, meaningful, and creative!

JASON

MATT

Yo! I'm Matthew. I'm curious about all kinds of things like...why can't I kiss the tip of my elbow? And, how can a fly walk on the ceiling? But right now, what I'm most curious about is scrapbooking. It looks neat—you get to use weird-looking tools and stuff— but I don't know how to get started. Help!

Scrapbooking is a way to preserve photos, memorabilia (cool stuff like postcards, ribbons and maps) and stories in a neat book. People have been putting together memory books for more than a hundred years, but today's scrapbooking is totally different because it's SAFE, MEANINGFUL and CREATIVE. It's also lots of fun!

LINDSAY

Never fear, Lindsay's here! I'm cool when it comes to scrapbooking. I've been doing it ever since I was a little kid. So, don't worry Matthew. I'll teach you what you need to know about the neatest hobby around. To begin with, creative scrapbooking is SAFE!

3

SAFE

Some papers, glues, pens and plastics damage photos. They make them turn colors and become brittle and old-looking. Or, they can cause them to stick to pages. That makes it tough if you ever want to remove them. Today's scrapbookers protect their photos by using "safe" products.

Look for album pages, paper, die cuts, stickers and glues that are labeled:

☼ Acid-free, lignin-free

Look for pens that are labeled:

☼ Permanent and light-fast

☼ Archival quality, acid-free

☼ Non-bleeding

☼ Waterproof

Look for plastic sleeves and page protectors that are labeled:

☼ PVC* free

Is ACID-FREE _really_ important?

You bet it is! Nice bright-colored paper will soon fade if there's acid in it! Photos that come in contact with acidic paper and glues can yellow or stain. Ish! So, look for the words, "acid-free" on the label.

* PVC or polyvinyl chloride is a chemically active plastic used for some album page protectors. BE CAREFUL, it will damage your photos. Look for PVC-free labels on albums!

Neutral 7 Acidic Identifier — Quickly identifies acid content of: •Stickers •Doilies •Stationery •Textile Products •Gessoed Canvas

If you are unsure of the acid content of the paper you're using, simply use the Nuetral 7 Pen. It "tests" products for acid— every scrapbooker should have one on hand!

Notice how an official time record, a ribbon, and a newspaper clipping make this a dynamite page. Make sure your memorabilia (which probably contains acid) does not come in contact with your snapshots. Copy newspaper articles on acid-free paper, because newsprint contains lignin or wood pulp which turns paper yellow, brown and brittle in a short time. Be a safe, smart scrapbooker— make an album that will last!

MEANINGFUL

Your scrapbook should scream, "This is who I am! This is what I think and feel and do!" Make your album one-of-a-kind, just like you. Be picky about what you include in your scrapbook.

Photos: Don't feel like you need to include every photo in your album. Choose the best shots and store the others. Look for favorite pictures that make you grin, think, laugh or remember.

When you select only the most special photographs and memorabilia, your scrapbook becomes more meaningful!

What is memorabilia? Memorabilia can include all kinds of just-gotta-keep-it stuff like: invitations, cards, announcements, report cards, school work, schedules, tickets, brochures, maps, ribbons, menus, drawings, letters, poems, sheet music, or baseball cards.
If you haven't been saving and collecting memorabilia, it's time to start. Include these mementos of special times to make a scrapbook to call your very own!

JGURN GIVES YO A

funky

cool

WOW!

Journaling adds kick to your album. Tell the story in your own words or borrow from the pros. Use your favorite song lyrics, poems, Bible verses, or quotes to make your pages speak.

There are lots of ways to journal, try them all!

Bullets supply only the basic information such as who, when, what and where. Ex: Lindsay, 10, First Swim Meet with YMCA Sharks, Venice, FL.

Captions put bulleted information into sentences. Ex: I swam in my first swim meet just a couple of days after I turned 10, in Venice, Florida. I was a member of the YMCA Sharks. I can't believe it. I won on my first try!

Storytelling includes the basic bullet-type of information but wraps it up in a story. It's easiest to storytell if you pretend like you're writing in your diary, or sharing some exciting news with your best friend.

EXAMPLE

ALING
ur ALBUM
VOICE

Ever since I was little I've loved the water! Mom says I even loved my bath, as well as running in puddles, and playing in the rain! I had my first swim lesson at 4, and learned to dog-paddle. When I was 10, my friend told me about the YMCA Sharks Swim Team. I begged Mom and Dad to let me try out. I made the team, but I had never competed before. I was so nervous at the first swim meet in Venice, Florida, that I had butterflies in my stomach. I was SO surprised when my lap time came in the lowest and I won!! Now, I realize I can do anything I put my mind to!

9

Safe and Meaningful are important reasons to scrapbook, but I'm into tools! There are things to cut, spin, trace, draw and punch. Too cool! With those tools and a scrapbook, I'm ready to be Creative!

CREATIVE

Having the ability to make or do something in a new way. Showing artistic inventiveness or imagination.

You are creative ... Take a minute and close your eyes and think of a good memory, like your last birthday. What do you see? Friends, cake, presents, colors? The pictures that appear in your mind's eye are formed by your imagination. Scrapbooking is a creative way to express those pictures. Through snapshots, words, colors and shapes, you can invent great pages and designs. The next few pages will teach you about "too cool tools" that you can be creative with. Then your imagination will have no limits!

pens

Zig® archival quality pens are available in dozens of colors and writing tips.

fancy rulers

Deja Views® Viewlers™ and Doodads™ come with decorative edges for tracing fancy border designs on paper .

paper edgers

Fiskars® Paper Edgers and Corner Edgers cut dozens of fancy patterns.

circle cutters

Fiskars® Circle Cutter™ cuts various size circles perfectly every time.

TOOCOOLSCRAPBOOKING

trimmers

Sturdy slicing machines like Fiskars® Portable Paper Trimmer make it possible to cut perfect straight edges on your paper and photos.

templates

Deja Views® plastic templates can be used to create great shapes from photos and papers.

punches

Marvy Uchida® paper punches are available in several sizes and lots of whimsical shapes.

die cuts

Fun and colorful paper shapes made with the Accu-Cut® system can be used in creative ways.

paper

Acid-free, lignin-free, archival quality papers come in a variety of colors and patterns.

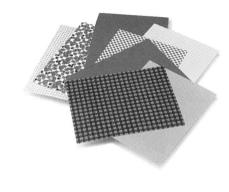

Crimpers

Nifty tools, like Fiskars® Paper Crimper™ "pleat" paper into accordion-like patterns.

TOOLSANDOTHERFUNSTUFF

photo corners

Mount photos on a page with "mini pockets" called corners. Try them in different colors.

stickers

Stickopotomus® wild and wonderful stickers add personality to pages!

adhesives

Acid-free glues in sticks and tubes, and special sticky squares make it possible to easily stick photos to a page.

Color Scrapbookers can choose from a rainbow of colored and patterned paper. Bright stickers, pens and die cuts also brighten up album pages. Use colors that help set the mood and tell the story. Red is an exciting color. Orange is a warm color. Yellow is a happy color. Green is a relaxing color. Blue is serene. Color can be an awesome creative tool to communicate your personality.

Shape Mixing shapes is a great way to add character and interest to a page. Cut photos and paper into all sorts of shapes, or create endless colorful designs with templates or die cuts. Flowers, apples, birds, baseball bats, fish...get crazy! Shape is where it's at!

Texture All paper isn't alike. Some papers feel smooth, while other paper is rough. Mix textures to give your album page depth. Or, use a crimper (one cool tool!) to put tiny folds in a sheet. Try embossing, you can feel the pattern under your fingers! Don't forget memorabilia such as napkins or awards. They can also help turn a flat page into something with texture!

Design Add pizzazz to your album! You don't have to just stack photos on a scrapbook page. Tip 'em. Crop 'em. Move 'em around. Mix shapes and sizes. Use fancy, decorative rulers to create borders. Wow 'em with color and texture. Go for a theme. Go wild. Get CREATIVE!

Templates are great! Try 'em and have a blast adding color, shape, and design to your scrapbook page.

CREATIVE PHOTOGRAPHY

Anybody who has a finger and a camera can take a picture, right? Right! But taking a GOOD picture is harder. You need to know the difference between using film and wasting it. You need to know how to center the objects in that little window. You need to know how to stop "fuzzy" photos before they happen. Good photographers know all of that and more. Here are some tips for making art with your camera; to make your memory album the best it can be!

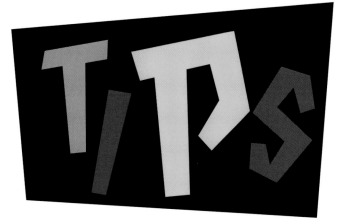

☼ Hold camera **VERY STEADY** while snapping button.

☼ Make sure you are **CLOSE ENOUGH TO YOUR SUBJECT.**

☼ Check the background— is it what you want?

☼ Is the sun at your back? (Pictures will not turn out if your camera faces the sun.)

☼ Keep spare batteries handy.

☼ If taking a picture of a group, make sure the people are close enough together for you to capture them **ALL** in your frame!

☼ Make sure no one is **MOVING.**

☼ Check for smiles — "Say cheese please!"

☼ Try picking up a panoramic or underwater disposable camera and experimenting with your photography.

☼ Stop spoooooky red-eye in pictures of people and pets by taking your photo at a slight angle.

If you do happen to get "red eye," use a Flash Out™ pen by Uchida to correct it and salvage your precious photograph.

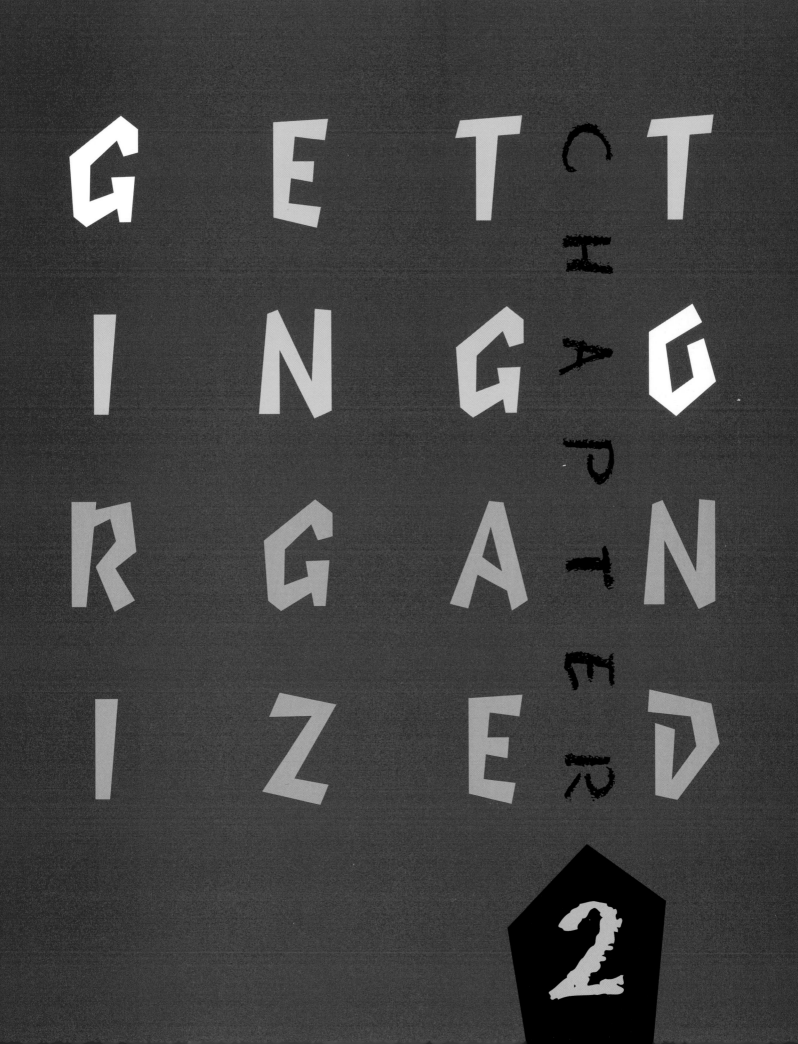

GETTING ORGANIZED

CHAPTER

2

Hauling boxes of stored photos is easier with a friend. Take the pictures to a well-lit area where you'll have plenty of room to work.

It's hard to create an album page that is Safe, Meaningful and Creative when your photos are mish-mashed in boxes, you can't find your memorabilia, and your supplies are scattered everywhere!   So, before you start on your scrapbooking project, you need to get organized. Don't worry, it's a lot easier than cleaning your room. Gathering, Sorting, Labeling, and Storing can be part of the scrapbooking fun!

GATHER PHOTOS

They're hiding and it's your job to find 'em! Maybe your mom or dad stored the "extra" photos in boxes and placed them in your closet attic, or basement. Ask the grown-ups for clues that will point you in the direction of those hidden pictures. Make sure you ask permission from Mom or Dad to use and cut photos.

SORT AND LABEL

It's time to open up those boxes of photos or go through the stacks. Get ready to laugh, groan, and have some fun. Sorting photos can take time, but while you do it you'll have a chance to look at every shot. Could that baby in the picture (the one with the sticky-outie ears) really be you?! How could your mom ever have worn those bell bottom pants and platform shoes? Did Dad really own a 1952 Willies Jeep. Too cool!

Sort the photos into piles. Put birthday pictures in a birthday stack, school pictures in a school stack, pictures of friends in a friend pile and stuff like that. Then re-sort the pictures in each stack; put the oldest pictures on the bottom and work your way up to today's shots.

I haven't seen this since I was a little kid!

Is that me?

If your folks aren't too keen about handing over the family photos, don't worry! Just borrow the pictures and have copies made at your neighborhood copy center. After you get your album "caught up," you'll want to add snapshots as they're developed to keep it up to date!

Collect your pens, rulers, scissors, and other tools. Seek and find your memorabilia (those sneaky ribbons, school papers, ticket stubs, and other things usually hidden in the backs of drawers and closets or under beds). Once you've gotten your stuff all together, you're ready to begin.

WRITE ON THE BACK OF EACH PICTURE WITH A SPECIAL PHOTO MARKER, OR ACID-FREE PEN.
(NEVER USE AN INK PEN!)

Special Photo Marking Pen

EXPOSURES®

Archival Acid-Free Pen

When you sort snapshots with a family member, it helps you remember the story behind them.

Don't forget to label your photos!

Put down the names of everyone in the shot, and then when and where it was snapped. Ask your mom or dad to help. If you're on your own, put on your detective hat. Search for clues in photos that will help you find information. Look at the age of the people in the picture. Study the background. Figure out the years of the cars. Pay attention to the style of clothes. Then make your best guess and write it on the back of the photo.

Oops, sorry, Lindsay, I didn't know.

Matthew, please be careful when you're handling photos. Even clean hands have oil on them that can hurt pictures, so hold them by their edges!

STORAGE

The safest place to store photos is in an acid-free, PVC-free scrapbook. But if your photos haven't made it into an album just yet, you need to keep them in an acid-free, PVC-free storage system. There are lots of different storage containers to consider like the photo or supply case by Cropper Hopper™. The supply case is also perfect for storing scrapbook tools. You will find a special spot for scissors, pens, punches, and glue sticks. The opposite side can hold paper, die cuts, or photos. If you're really into scrapbooking, use Cropper Hopper's Scrapbook Tote to store everything you own, including your albums, camera, rulers, trimmer and circle cutter. The Scrapbook Tote has all sorts of neat little custom-sized compartments and pockets for your "stuff" so you can get and stay organized!

Where have you been? I've been waiting to talk to you about storing your photos and tools. When I began scrapbooking I used to keep my stuff in holes I dug in the backyard. Not a great idea. The photos got soggy when it rained and the scissors rusted. So I sniffed around and came up with some better ways to keep my supplies. I'll tell you about them.

SCRAPBOOKING FOR KIDS

PUTTING THE

CHAPTER 3

PIECES

TOGETHER

CROPPING

Don't go crazy with cropping, Matthew. Once a photo has been cropped it can't be UN-cropped so think hard before you start to snip. Remember, not all pictures need to be cropped. And don't, no matter how much fun you're having, crop old historical photos. You don't want to get rid of that great stuff in the background, like a 1930 Ford!

ƒ you enjoyed cutting your doll's hair or were one of those kids who drove your teachers crazy by slicing the edge of your papers into brooms you're going to loooove cropping! Cropping means cutting a photo into a different size or shape. It can be used to make the picture more interesting or more balanced. It can also remove the uh-oh's (the camera strap, your thumb, dark backgrounds, or unknown people) from a shot.

There are lots of different ways to crop your photos.
A trimmer is a tool that cuts clean, straight edges.
Cropping with a trimmer is as easy as 1-2-3!

Stuff You Need
Photo
Fiskars Portable
  Paper Trimmer
Adhesive

Cropping With A Trimmer

Step 1 ▷

Raise the trimmer's "ruler arm" and place the photo on trimmer so that the photo edge you want to cut is along the trimmer's cutting line. Lower the ruler arm.

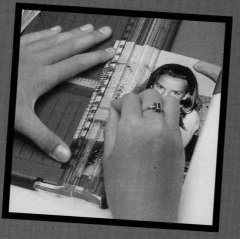

△ Step 2

Hold down the ruler arm with your left hand so the photo doesn't wiggle away. Don't let go!

△ Step 3

Push down the trimmer blade button with your right hand and slide the blade through the photo. Don't stop sliding until the whole picture is cut.

What a tidy job! ▷

LEFT-HANDED?

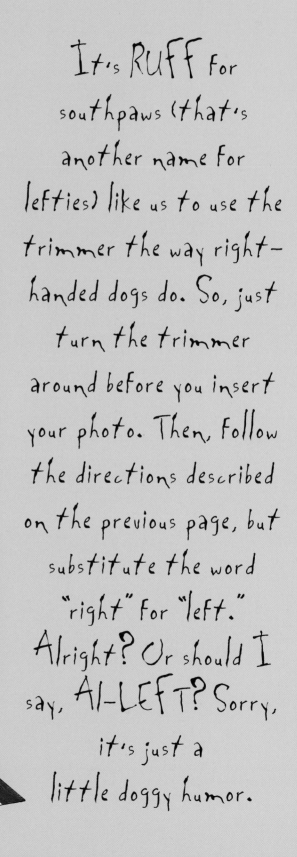

Woof! You're on the cutting edge with a little trimmer!

It's RUFF for southpaws (that's another name for lefties) like us to use the trimmer the way right-handed dogs do. So, just turn the trimmer around before you insert your photo. Then, follow the directions described on the previous page, but substitute the word "right" for "left." Alright? Or should I say, AI-LEFT? Sorry, it's just a little doggy humor.

Silhouette Cropping

Pop goes the picture when you silhouette crop! All it takes is a pair of scissors, a steady hand, and a special photo to create a picture that seems to leap off the page.

△ Step 1
Have a great picture with a not-so-great background? It's a perfect photo to silhouette crop.

△ Step 2
Carefully...oh so carefully, cut around the edge of the main subject. You don't want to trim off a nose! Then throw the part you trimmed off away.

△ Step 3
Stick the cropped photo on brightly colored paper. See what you can do? Wow!

Stuff You Need
Photo
Scissors
Paper

Silhouetted photos come alive on the page, sorta like a 3-D effect!

Cropping With Templates

Everybody needs a little help sometimes and a template makes it easy to cut photos into perfect shapes. There are hundreds of plastic templates to chose from. Some have funky bordered edges to trace with, and punched holes for easy storage in a 3-ring binder.

Yeah, that's what they all say, but I can see right through you.

◁ Step 1

Place your template over the photo so the best part of the picture looks through the hole.

△ Step 2

Trace around the inside edge of the template.

△ Step 3

Remove the template and carefully cut along the traced line. You've created a perfectly cropped photo!

Great Job!

There is an excitement and specialness about sleepovers with best friends. You can share your thoughts, secrets, dreams (and popcorn). You can cook up fun snacks and goodies and play all kinds of games or just simply be together. Don't forget, scrapbooking is extra fun when you do it with a friend, and where better then at a sleepover ... share memories and snap shots!

Cropping With Mix 'n Mats

Mix 'n Mats are nifty templates that make it possible to crop photos which will fit together on a page kinda like a jigsaw puzzle! You may have to play around a bit before you find the perfect photos that fit in the template windows. Keep in mind that photos with the same theme work best on one page.

Step 2 ▷
Use next larger size template (same or different shape) to trace and cut a paper shape.

Step 3 ▷
Glue photo to brighter color coordinated paper and trim.

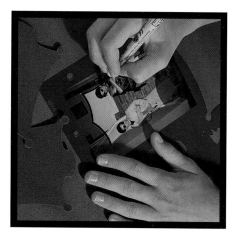

△ Step 1
Place photos under smaller Mix 'n Mat template. Wiggle them around until they peek through the windows just right. Trace inside the template borders, then cut carefully around trace lines.

Step 4 ▷
Adhere cut and matted photo to larger template paper shape.

Step 5 ▷

If you wish, trace the template border design around the outside edge of your paper. Trim for a decorative look. Decorate and journal your scrapbook page.

You've Mix 'n Matted to make perfectly cropped pages!

Matting

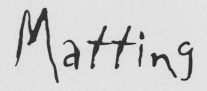

Photos look snappier when they're framed. When you make paper frames to put behind your album pictures it's called MATTING.

Step 1 ▷
Pick a paper that looks good with your photo.

Step 2 ◁
Stick the photo on the paper with glue Make sure that at least 1/2 inch of paper shows all around the photo.

Step 3 ▷
Trim away the extra paper so there's an even frame all around the shot.

Step 4 ◁
Way to go!

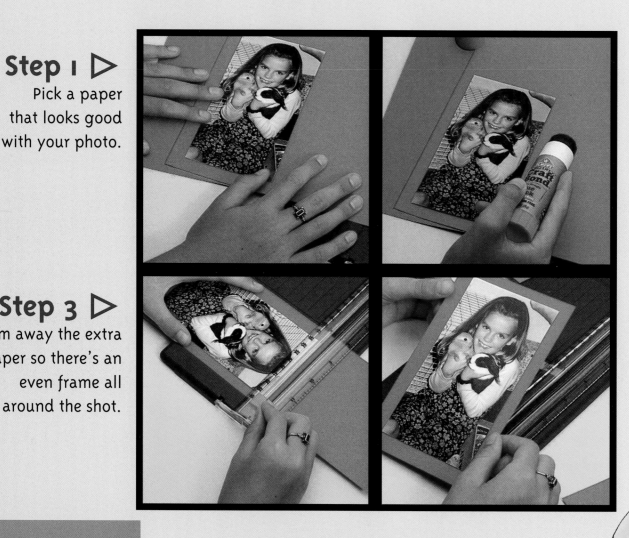

Stuff You Need
Trimmed photo
Acid-free paper
Fiskars Portable
  Paper Trimmer
Adhesive

Lindsay says to crop your photos before you mat them. Then get ready for some fun. Matting is really cool. That's why it's called Matt-ing. (Uh-oh, I'm starting to sound like that crazy dog.)

Double Matting

Stuff You Need
Trimmed photo
Acid-free paper
Fiskars Portable
   Paper Trimmer
Adhesive (or try
   adhesive paper)

Make fancier "Double" mats by matting the photo you just matted. Confused? Don't worry. There's nothing to it, especially when you use adhesive papers.

Step 1 ▷

Glue your matted picture onto a larger sheet of colored paper, (or just peel and stick If you're using adhesive paper). Again, trim to 1/2 inch all the way around the edge.

Step 2 ▷

Voila! An eye-catching double mat! Try it! Mix in a variety of colored paper combinations for different effects.

What a tidy job!

Lindsay

HAPPY BIRTHDAY TO YOU, HAPPY BIRTHDAY TO YOU, HAPPY BIRTHDAY DEAR LINDSAY, HAPPY

Birthday Book

HONEY
ROSIE
AND ME!

There's nothing
sweeter in all the
world than snuggling
with my BUNNIES!

Make your matting really matter. Use one of these nifty methods to turn your mats into works of art.

Paper Edgers (or Decorative Scissors)

Cut around your mats with a pair of cool Fiskars Paper Edgers. There are dozens of patterns to choose from, which offer you endless creative choices! Have fun deciding which ones to use first.

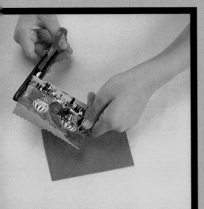

◁ Step 1

Be creative and use paper edgers on your photos.

Step 2 ▷

You can cut a fancy edge around your mats, too. Be sure to re-align your scissors' edge exactly into your prior cut each time. This ensures a "clean cut."

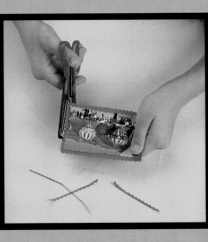

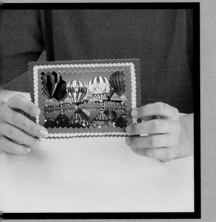

◁ Step 3

Wow! What a neat effect! It's a custom-made mat, and you did it all by yourself!

Stuff You Need
Trimmed photo
Paper in 2 different colors
Fiskars Paper Edgers
(scallop shown here)
Adhesive

◁ **Step 1**

Insert paper or photo into either of the two notched edges and cut. (You can flip the edger over to get two more unique cuts.)

Step 2 ▷

Use the corder edger on the corners of your photos as well as your colored mats.

Corner Edgers

Fiskars Corner Edgers aren't quite scissors, and not quite a corner punch. They are a nifty tool that you can use to jazz up the corners of mats and snapshots. Each Corner Edger can produce four different cuts. You can create double, triple, or quadruple mats with contrasting colors! Save your corner cuts to get really cool looks—stack them, use them for corner accents, or make corner patterns for your pages. Use your imagination! There are several different Corner Edgers to choose from.

Stuff You Need
Photo
Fiskars Corner Edgers
Paper
Adhesive

Here's an example of four possible cuts when using just <u>one</u> Corner Edger!

Corner Rounders

Stuff You Need
Trimmed photo
Marvy Uchida Corner
   Rounder
Paper
Fiskars Portable
   Trimmer
Adhesive

Corner rounders and punches carve the corners of photos or mats into different shapes. They are easy to use.

Step 1 ▷

Slip corner rounder over trimmed photo corner. Be sure to hold the photo in place while you cut the corner! Hold firmly and use thumb to push down button.

◁ Step 2

Stick your corner rounded photo onto a colored paper and trim.

△ Step 4

Just like that, you've got a well-rounded page!

Step 3 ▷

Now, use your corner rounder to round the corners of your paper mat!

Try tearing a sun, starfish or a few waves!

Look what you can do when you add
just a little torn paper to a page!

Mounting

Don't 'cha just love it? It's a great time to get organized with mounted photos. Don't get frustrated with an album that flutters out photos and memorabilia like a snow storm when you pick it up. Now that you've learned to crop and mat, it's time to learn to mount your pictures and other stuff safely in your book!

Put an end to flutter-about (when photos come flying out of your album). Use a high-quality glue or adhesive.

No question about it, you want your photos, papers, and memorabilia to *stay* in your scrapbook. So, apply one of the nifty new photo-safe adhesives directly on the back of the photo or mat. Or, apply easy-to-use adhesive squares. Place the sticky photo or mat onto the album page, press and smooth. That's all it takes to permanently mount all your materials.

Non-Permanent Mounting

Some photos may just "visit" your album for a while. Then they're off to other exciting places (like your sister's album or the photo copy shop). A good example is old family history photographs. When you're not sure that a picture it going to settle in, use a non-permanent mounting technique like photo corners to secure it.

Photo corners are nifty "pockets" into which you slip the corners of your (you guessed it) photo! The photo corners are then stuck to the mat and not your photo! That means that you can gently remove your snapshot. Photo corners come in lots of styles and colors to go with your favorite pictures.

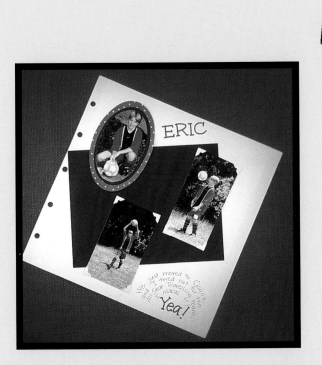

Pocket Pages

Photos and memorabilia can be held in your album inside envelope-type pockets that you make yourself. They can be fancy or simple. Just follow these instructions.

Stuff You Need
Accu-Cut or Canson die cut shapes
2 sheets paper
2 scrapbook pages
Scissors
Adhesive
Stuff to put inside

Step 1 ▷
First, add colorful die cuts to a piece of paper.

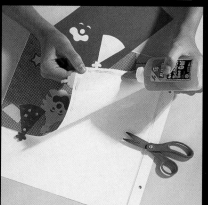

◁ Step 2
Next, glue the paper to a scrapbok page.

Step 3 ▷
Cut into scrapbook page, and around the die cuts. This is your "pocket."

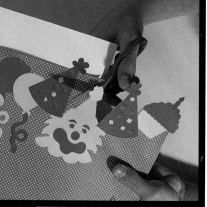

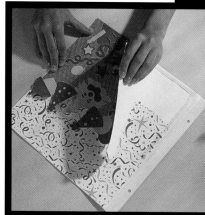

◁ Step 4
Glue a sheet of decorative paper to top half of second scrapbook page. Then, glue your "pocket" to bottom half.

△ Step 5
Mount the pocket page inside your album and slip your stuff inside. You can add die cut letters for pizzazz. Super cool!

50

CHAPTER 4

Letter Perfect

YOUR SCRAPBOOK IS AN EXPRESSION OF WHO YOU ARE. ALL YOUR PAGES ARE KEEPERS.

Don't worry

about your penmanship. You don't have to have perfect handwriting! Use creative lettering to journal, label, and title your way through your album. You'll find that the more you write, the more right your lettering will look! You have the "write stuff!"

GATHER YOUR LETTERING SUPPLIES

- ☼ Mechanical or #2 pencil
- ☼ Soft white or art gum eraser
- ☼ Ruler and/or templates
- ☼ acid-free, pigment ink, non-bleeding pens in assorted tips and colors
- ☼ Paper to practice

Dual Tip

Go on! Keep reading. I'm gonna give you a cat's-eye view of more creative ways to letter. Wait a minute—did I say, "cat's-eye?" Uh-oh, one more slip like that and I'll end up in the doghouse for sure!

PRACTICE MAKES PERFECT

Practice a bit on scratch paper before you write directly in your album. Play with different styles and sizes of letters. Do it all again with different colored inks and pen tips. Some pens have a dual tip (two pens in one); a fine tip on one end and a handy bullet tip on the other! Cut out the practice words and position them on your album page. Move them around until they look just right. Now you know where to put the "real" lettered words when you write directly on the scrapbook page.

PICK A PRINT

By changing the height, width, size, and shape of letters you can give your words a whole new look. Think of it as a fashion makeover for the alphabet. abcdefg Letters can be stretched, hijkl squashed, mnopq fattened, rstuv or put on a diet! wxyz

LETTERING IDEAS

Celebrate

Kiss Me

·i LOVE·MY·PUPPY·

WINTER

Sleep-Over

It was the best PARTY of the year!

Grandma

hip-hip-hooray!

USA

HAPPY BIRTHDAY!!

SLUMBER PARTY

The best FAMILY ever!!

KISS the COOK

A friend is a FOREVER thing !

FOND MEMORIES

FRIENDSHIP

Warms the heart

Family Reunion

ALL STAR ATHLETE

back to school

Shall we Dance?

Going to school is really COOL

BASKETBALL

our Summer Vacation

LOVE

CRAZY DAYS

on top of the world

YEAH!

what a BLAST!

Grandma's are just Moms with lots of practice!

COLORADO

we love ANIMALS

Spring

Hoppy Easter JORDAN

Soccer

Beachcombing

FAMILY FUN

Lindsay's 10th Birthday

I LOVE SPORTS

Kori

Sisters are forever friends!

ERIC'S BIG GAME

The Story of A CHAMPION

What a Show-off!

Dear Old Dad!

Summer

Fourth of July

I love Tennis!

CREATIVE

Aa Bb Cc Dd Ee
Ff Gg Hh Ii Jj Kk
Ll Mm Nn Oo Pp
Qq Rr Ss Tt Uu
Vv Ww Xx Yy Zz

Aa Bb Cc Dd Ee Ff Gg
Hh Ii Jj Kk Ll Mm Nn
Oo Pp Qq Rr Ss Tt Uu Vv
Ww Xx Yy Zz
1234567890 ?!$

ALPHABETS

AaBbCcDdEeFf
GgHhIiJjKkLl
MmNnOo PpQq
RrSsTtUuVv
WwXxYyZz
1234567890?!$

aBCDEfgHij
KLMhOPQRS
tuVWXyZ

→ Lettering created with Pebbles Funky Tracer

THE
JOURNALING GENIE

Looking for help decorating your one-of-a-kind pages? All you'll need is your very own personal genie. This template makes fancying-up your album pages just a wish away. Use a pencil and your Journal Genie to trace squiggles, wavy lines, or spirals. Then, write above the lines with a marker. When you're done, just erase the pencil lines. Like magic, you'll have pages you can be extra proud of!

We went to Disneyworld this summer. My cousins Eric, Joel and Sarah came too. We had a BLAST!

I HAVE A DOG NAMED MAGGIE. I LOVE HER VERY MUCH. SHE IS A SCOTTISH TERRIER. I'VE HAD HER FOR 2 YEARS. SHE'S A SWEET DOG.
woof! woof! growl! growl! woof! woof! arf! arf!

Journaling Genie

→ My 10th birthday was Awesome☆ This year I had a pool party. All of my friends came. We played water basket-ball & volleyball. It was totally cool!

to make brownies. I can't wait!

said that I'm the only person in the WHOLE world that she's ever shared it with.

In JUNE I went to GRANDMA'S house and we made the BEST oatmeal cookies ever with her SECRET recipe. She

←EXAMPLE

🐝 I MADE A NEW FRIEND AT CAMP THIS YEAR. HER NAME IS LISA. WE WON THE CANOE RACE TOGETHER AND LEARNED TO MAKE A FIRE WITHOUT USING ANY MATCHES 🐝

JOURNALING WITH TEMPLATES

We saw the coolest rainbow on our way to the lake. We stopped to play in the rain and take pictures! How pretty is that?

Templates come in hundreds of shapes from funky to fun. Choose one that works with your page theme. Hold the template firmly in place on the album page. Gently trace around the template. Remove the template. Journal inside or along the outside of the traced lines.

You can create "word pictures" with templates by holding them down and journaling tightly inside. Or, trace templates with a pencil, remove and write along traced edge. Imagine all the possibilities.

Everyone ♡'s DOGS

Our vacation at the beach was so cool...we got great tans...went snorkeling every day...ate tons of seafood (yum!) and enjoyed being together!

When I count my blessings, the greatest of my joys, Our parents gave us SIBLINGS instead of rooms of toys!

I LOVE MY FAMILY

We were so excited to be the CHAMPIONS! My friend Bob was the anchor, and did a great job. We were so excited! Our team had the fastest time! My friend Bob was AWESOME! The ropes course at camp Id-Ra-Ha-Je was AWESOME!

CHAPTER 5

DIE CUT TIPS AND TRICKS

Die cuts are to drool over! Just be careful. The tricky adhesive ones can sneak up on you when your tail is turned. Then before you know it someone's yanking them off you and throwing around that "B" word (bath).

Die cuts are one of the easiest, fastest ways to turn a ho-hum page into a traffic-stopper. They come in hundreds of shapes and colors. Some stores have die cut machines you can use to cut your own from adhesive-backed paper. Then you just peel and stick your shapes to decorate your page.

Have fun! Get creative!

HERE ARE A FEW DIE CUT TIPS TO GET YOUR "CREATIVE JUICES" FLOWING!

OUR FISHING TRIP

Add words over a die cut.

LAKEWOOD ELEMENTARY
1st day of school

MY PHONE # IS (942) 368-501

Combine with cut ruler designs.
Add texture with pen!

Write on a die cut!

Cut, mix and combine colors of die cuts.

Cut in half!

Die cuts: those wacky, wonderful (and sometimes even weird) decorative paper shapes, make great backgrounds for creative lettering. Either write directly on the die cut, or journal around the edges. The colored die cut will draw your eye to the words again and again.

S-T-R-E-T-C-H YOUR IMAGINATION.

Use in multiples and layer! A forest of trees, a herd of moose or deer, a school of fish, flock of birds, bunches of leaves, bouquets of flowers, etc.

► Layer on colored pieces of paper for dimension and detail.

Journal inside! ▼

GOLDIE is the best kitty ever! We got her when she was really tiny, and she's grown up to be a big, fluffy, Wonderful pet!!

Add sticker
► letters.

► Crimp a pencil, leaf, can of worms...

NO. 2

Add contrasting pen to letters to make them stand out! ▼

Use fancy scissors on letter shapes and back with contrasting colors.

My first airplane ride was such a blast! I got to sit by the window and watch the city disappear under the clouds. I spotted a movie and eat dinner. The landing made me a little nervous, but I'm ready to fly again!

S P O R T S

LOVE

SETH

Combine die cut shapes: confetti and kitty.

▲ Add stickers to die cut letters for a cool title on your scrapbook page!

Back letters with patterned paper. ▲

▲ Use theme related stickers to make your die cut letters "shout" their meaning.

◄Make► creative borders using rulers, scissors, and die cut shapes!

Think of punched shapes as mini die cuts. Use them in multiples, layers, borders, or alone on your scrapbook page! It's dog gone fun!

To do simple borders, just punch out your favorite shapes from paper and combine them with drawn ruler edges.

PUNCHES ARE JUST MINI DIE CUTS!

Don't Bug Me! Don't Bug Me!

A circle cut in half makes a lady bug.

Two hearts cut at an angle make a butterfly.

Layer circles to do a caterpillar.

Combine punched shapes and stickers.

Merry Christmas Merry Christmas Merry

Combine theme-related punched shapes!

STRAWBERRY FIELDS FOREVER STRAWBERRY FIELDS

Punch out shapes from patterned papers!

CHAPTER 6

BORDERS

What is a border? Well, a border is a decorated edge or trim you can add to the edges of your scrapbook page. Simple borders are easy and quick when you use decorative rulers and pens. All you need is imagination and a steady hand!

RULER BORDERS

Use the decorative edge of your favorite ruler to create all kinds of fancy borders. If you're feeling fancy, draw some words or doodles. Or, use a ruler to trace a pattern on colored paper. Then, cut the pieces out to use as borders.

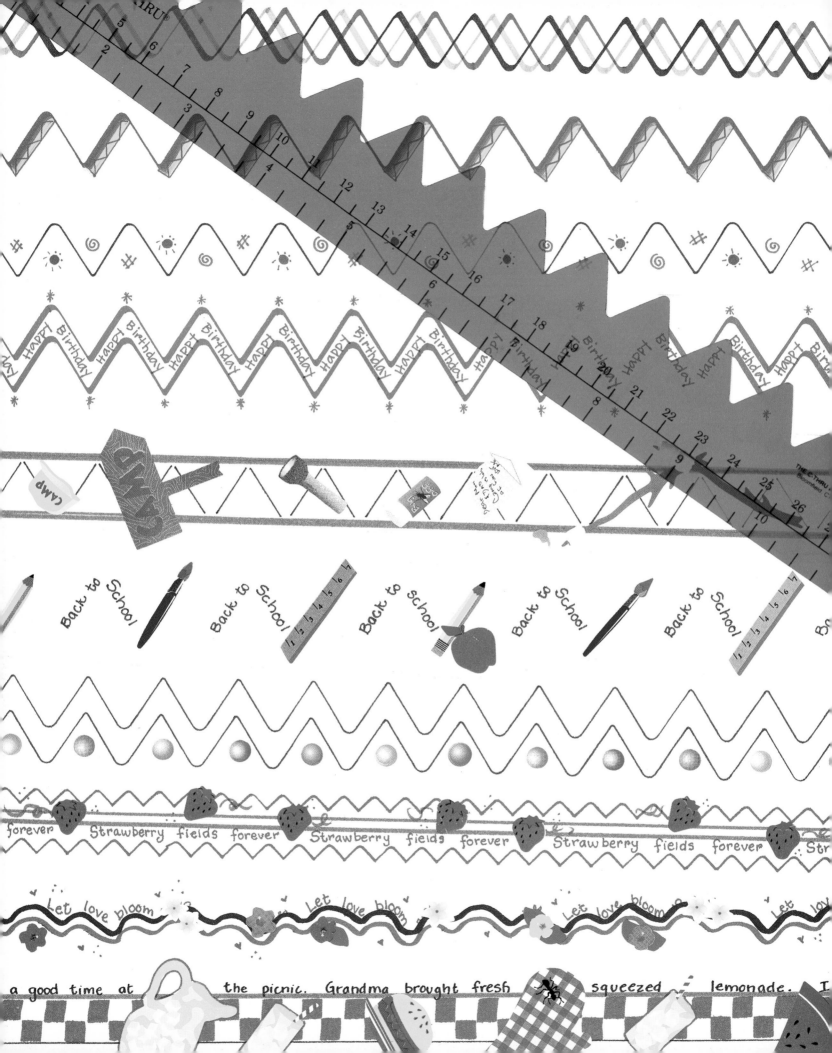

A Doodad

is a funky ruler you can use to help draw borders. Doodads are a perfect combination of ruler and stencil! Collect them and you're on your way to making awesome scrapbook pages.

What is a DOODAD?

Stuff You Need
Pencil
Photos
Paper
Fiskars Wave Paper Edgers
Straight-edged scissors
The Journaling Genie
Accu-Cut die cut letters
Deja Views Viewlers
(Rulers)
Zig acid-free pen
Adhesive (optional)

Paper and Ruler Borders

Get crazy with colored paper and your favorite rulers. Make borders that add snap to your page!

Step 1 ▷

Trace wave ruler design on paper.

Step 2 ▷

Cut along the traced line with straight-edge scissors. Adhere wave to bottom of page.

Step 3 ▷

Trim photo edges with decorative wave-patterned scissors. Trim adhesive papers into mats with same scissors.

◁ Step 4

Stick mats to page and glue photos on top. Trace ruler on paper and cut along traced lines. Snip off pointy tips and save the pieces.

◁ Step 5

Use the Journaling Genie to draw spirals on paper with pencil. Journal along drawn lines.

Erase pencil marks. Adhere previously cut triangular tips (trimmed off in Step 4) around spiraled journaling to create sun-like design.

◁ Step 6

Dad and I went on a cruise when I was seven years old. I think I saw a SHARK!

...All geared up and ready!

One day we rented jet skis. What a blast! We went to grandpa and grandma's house on Cayuga Lake in Minnesota. Matthew, Dad and I had a great summer vacation in July, 1998. Cousin Kristin, Matthew, brady

Jet Ski

Cousin Kristin

Stickopota
BINDER STICK

You can cut ruler designs out of your photos, too!
It almost looks like a real wave!

CHAPTER SEVEN

FINISHING TOUCHES

Rubber Stamps

How many do you own? Come on, confess! Most kids have rubber stamp collections that make their parents' favorite collection look puny! You can get rubber stamps of animals, shapes, letters, numbers, and more; (even your own name). Use your stamps to create scrapbook borders or plop down an image like a beauty mark next to your favorite photo. Decorate mats and pages with birthday, sports, vacation, or holiday stamps to match your snapshots. Just be careful. Once you've stamped your book, it's there forever. Make sure you use a "safe" ink pad with acid-free or pigment ink.

Stuff You Need
Rubber stamps (Fiskars Stacker Stamps shown)
Fiskars acid-free ink pad
Paper or scrapbook page

Step 1 ▷

Dab your stamp on the ink pad. Check to see if the stamp is evenly covered. Wet areas will look shiny.

Use your stamp collection if you have one. Remember to use a safe, acid-free ink pad.

Step 2 △

Press the stamp down on your page. Don't wiggle it around because the picture will blur. Lookin' good! Pick stamps to match your theme!

Embossing with Rubber Stamps

Rubber stamps are too cool all by themselves. But, if you want to go from cool to **COOLEST** try embossing your rubber stamp images. Embossing actually raises up your rubber creation and lets it shine! Here's what you do:

◁ Step 1

Stamp your design using a special embossing ink pad. The image will appear slightly shiny.

Step 2 ▷

Next, sprinkle embossing powder on the stamped image while the ink is still wet.

◁ Step 3

Shake off the extra powder.

Step 4 ▷

Ask a grown-up to hold the embossing gun. This heats the powder to make it shine!

Use a safe embossing heat tool like Marvy Uchida's with a plastic sleave over the metal nozzle.

85

SCRAPBOOKING FOR KIDS

Paper Embossing

Awesome emboss'n is cool! Embossing can give your scrapbook page dimension and texture—kinda like special effects in a movie, it looks really cool!

Embossing with a Stylus

To do embossing, you use this thing called a stylus. It's sorta like a pen with no ink. To emboss with a stylus, it's best to use a light box (you can find them at office supply and art stores). Place a template or ruler on the light box and tape your paper to it so it doesn't wiggle around. Just trace the shape completely by pressing down into the template with the stylus tool. When you're done, remove the paper and take a look at your very own "special effect".

Stuff You Need
Light box
Embossing Stylus tool
Paper
Brass or plastic template (Pebbles Funky Tracer shown here)
Tape
Wax Paper
Straight-edged scissors

△ **Step 1**

Place template on light box. Tape paper over the letter or design you want to emboss.

△ **Step 2**

Tear off a small piece of wax paper, crinkle it and rub over the item you are going to emboss.

△ **Step 3**

Trace over the design with a stylus. (Wax paper helps stylus glide smoothly). Press down firmly. Trace <u>completely</u> before removing tape and paper.

△ **Step 4**

On this page, we cut around the embossed letters and adhered them to the page with punched hearts. (See opposite).

Circle Cutter

Have you ever tried to cut a perfect circle? Tricky, huh? A circle cutter, like Fiskars Circle Cutter, is a tool you can use to cut accurate circles every time! Don't forget, they can be used to cut photos as well as paper, but practice on paper first.

☼ Circle cutters are easy to use for left or right handers.

☼ A cutting mat comes with the Fiskars Circle Cutter.

☼ Always make sure you have completely cut around the entire circle shape before lifting the tool.

☼ Use the Circle Cutter to make frames. (Cut larger circle first, then cut smaller circle inside.)

Stuff You Need
Photos
Fiskars Circle Cutter
(with mat)
Paper

SCRAPBOOKING FOR KIDS

There is no better way to cut a perfect circle! Try it!

CHAPTER

PROJECTS

AND

PAGES

8

ALL MY ADORABLE PETS

Come on. All together now,
"A h h h h h h h h h h."

There's just something awesome about a fuzzy, furry animal that makes you want to "oooooo" and "ahhhhh"; to cuddle it like a baby. Of course, not all pets are fluff balls. Some of the weirdest ones are scaly with googly eyes. No matter which type of animal turns you to mush, you'll want to capture it on film. Take your favorite photos and create an animal album, (or at least several pages), one that's as special as your adorable pet.

What an awesome pet!

"Yikes! He's kissing me!"

My little brother liked him, too!

Spike the iguaNa

COOKIN' UP SOMETHIN' SPECIAL

One way to always remember how to make great grandma's delicious lemon bars is to write the recipe directly on your scrapbook page. Better yet, include a recipe card handwritten by Grams herself!

Think rich milk chocolate. Think crusty hot bread. Think homemade apple pie. Now swallow hard and start thinking about how to record your cooking experiences in your scrapbook! Start by including photos of you and your friends chopping, stirring, and giggling in the kitchen. Put in pictures of your cooking masterpieces. Also include a few of your flops. Family recipes and your memories of family feasts help make a well-balanced book. Put the icing on the cake (so to speak) with mouth-watering stickers and die cuts. Bon Appetite!

Your friends will be eating their hearts out over your cooking pages. If you really get into cooking, you may find that you have enough pages to fill a whole scrapbook album! Why not photo copy the pages and make a gift scrapbook for your aunt or grandma?

94

COLLECTOR'S ALBUM

Collections come in all shapes and sizes, some old and some new. Many are worth a lot of money, while the value of others lies in sentiment. Whether your collectables are stamps, sports cards, postcards or something unique, it is sure to be one of your prized possessions! That's why it's worth the time to make sure it's stored safely in a scrapbook.

Collections are most easily viewed when organized and sorted. You may wish to sort stamps by date, theme or country of origin. Sports cards can be organized by team, sport, or even alphabetically by player for easy reference.

Mount, display and handle your collections carefully. Cover the pages with PVC-free page protectors to keep fingerprints and soil from damaging your collection and depreciating it's value.

Use an album that allows you to add new pages as you find new pieces to add to your collection. Your scrapbook, and your hobby, will continue to grow right along with your interest!

Only touch the stamps with clean, dry paws or you may find yourself with a sticky problem. And don't forget to use page protectors in your album. You'll want to keep these puppies clean.

TWO BITS, FOUR BITS, SIX BITS, A DOLLAR
ALL FOR BASEBALL STAND UP AND HOLLER!

Wait a minute. Some of you aren't hollering. Is it because you're not a baseball fan? Well, don't worry. Just take the word "baseball" out of the cheer and put in the name of the sport that makes you want to cheer.

BE A SPORT

My First Rockies Game.

I wore my Rockies cap and my Rockies t-shirt. for good luck... It must have worked because THEY WON !

Whether you spend your weekends on the field, on the pitchers mound, or in the bleachers, you're a sports fan. Keep track of those game highlights in your scrapbook sports pages. Along with those action shots and team portraits; you can include pictures of the winning scoreboard, trophies, ceremonies, and after-game pizza parties. Don't forget to put memorabilia like programs and tickets in your album.

Or, give your coach a gift album. Get your teammates to donate photos of games and practices. Ask each player to write the coach a short thank you note to be included in the book. Make a special "autographs only" page for team members to sign. Include autographs of professional players if possible! This book is sure to hit a home run with your coach and teammates.

PERSONAL HISTORY ALBUM

While our personalities are affected by experiences, much of who we are is also influenced by genes. Genes are a gift from our ancestors. They help decide our looks and basic make-up. When we get to know our ancestors, we get to know ourselves. And, when we understand more about why they chose to immigrate, marry, and worship like they did, we understand why we are where we are and why we do what we do.

Get to know yourself a bit better by getting to know your ancestors a LOT better. It takes some detective work to put together a personal history album, but snooping can be fun. Begin by hunting down old family photos and memorabilia. Then grab your tape recorder or a pen and start collecting family stories. You can write to the National Archives in Washington, D.C. or call your library and request information regarding a local genealogical society. You can contact them for ideas on how to get started delving into your family tree. Put on your detective hat and get ready to investigate. Send "question forms" to far-away relatives. (Make copies of the one on the next page.)

Dear ....

I am researching my family tree and need your help. Could you please take a few minutes to fill out this form and return it in the enclosed stamped envelope? I would also love to borrow any photographs or memorabilia you think I may find interesting. I will duplicate them and send the originals back to you immediately. This is really important to me because I am putting together my own family history album! I can't wait to see what you send!

Your Name: ....
Date and Place of Birth: ....
Spouse's Name: ....
Date and Place of Marriage: ....
Children's Names: ....
Children's Dates and Places of Birth: ....

Now comes the fun part. Can you tell me some stories? Here are ways you may start (but do it any way you want to):

When I was a child...
My parents loved to take us...
Every year my family would...
We lived...
I met my spouse...
I remember my grandparents. They were...
The most exciting thing that ever happened to me was...
Once, I got in BIG trouble...
Nobody knows this but...
I was part of history...

Can you draw your family tree on the back of this paper? Go back as far as you can.

Thank you, again, for helping me! If you have the names of other family members please send them to me so I can contact them!

TEEN MEMORIES

There is nobody in the world who looks like you. There is nobody who has all of the same experiences that you have. There is nobody who thinks exactly like you. And, there is nobody anywhere who feels about everything the way you do. As you become a teenager, you begin to take more notice of the world around you. And, in doing so, you grow more aware of how much of an individual you are. Celebrate the You-ness of you in your very own teen memories album.

The teen years are filled with special moments you're sure to capture on film. There are church youth group activities, best friend sleepovers, camps, sports clinics, clubs, school activities, boy/girlfriends, drama recitals, dances, football games, graduation, milestones, trips, your first drivers license, and the prom! Design a scrapbook filled with these shots and wrapped in your personality. Use the colors that turn you on. Feature the subjects you're most interested in.

Kirsten.

The most important part of a teen memories album may be the journaling. Use these pages to write down your deepest thoughts and feelings. List your favorite songs, dances, books, Bible verses, classes, movies, hangouts, and afterschool jobs. In addition to family and friends, include other special people in your life such as teachers, mentors, coaches, and neighbors. Write your hopes and dreams.

The album you create will be as unique as the person who designed it.

SCHOOL DAYS

Good old school days. There was so much to do, so much to learn. There were so many people to meet and enjoy! Quick! Before you forget the names of classmates, or the school cheer you'd better start a school days album!

A school days scrapbook is the perfect place to put report cards, those papers with the gold stars, snapshots of school field trips, certificates, program brochures, artwork, and the words to the school song. Don't forget to include the autographs and phone numbers of best friends.

If you're working on an ongoing school scrapbook, why not keep a disposable camera in your locker? You can whip it out to take shots of assemblies, school parties, and the unexpected crazy things that happen in and around the classroom. Dress up the pages with alphabet die cuts and apple stickers. Your book is sure to get an "A" for awesome!

CAR TRIP KEEPSAKE

You stare out the window hour after hour watching trees and cows flash by...and flash by...and flash by. Car trips can be BORING! The key to keeping a car trip exciting is to organize a project. And, one of the best projects to organize is your very own car trip scrapbook.

A car trip scrapbook is the place to hold photos you snap as you pause at interesting rest stops or lookout points. Include shots of activities inside the car (your sister or brother snoring away, the dog gazing out the window) as well as funny signs or interesting sights outside the car. Ask your parents to drop off your film at a one-hour developing center while you all eat lunch.

Take photos of buildings, mountains, parks, oceans, hotels, activities, events, new friends, family members, signs, distant relatives, and famous sites.

COLORADO VACA

We spent the day up at Lost Lake ~ fishing, hiking, and having a picnic.

It was such a treat to have the Min...

"Oh, deer!..."

Checkin' out ...Pass!

J.D.

I went to stay with my Aunt and Uncle in Colorado. The Fall colors were just perfect. I loved taking pictures of everything.

The Nature of Things

Dear Mom & Dad,
...the mountains are so cool! I think the colors are really pretty. We are having so much fun. I have taken alot of great pictures! Love,
Your daughter
P.S. miss you!!

A really cool old tree by the river.

A river at the bottom of a canyon.

TRUCK YS-54570 PENNSYLVANIA 2-95

ELMERS Craft Bond Glue Stick

ZIG OPAQUE WRITER

SEP FLORIDA

Don't forget to include memorabilia like:

restaurant menus
postcards
newspaper clippings
travel folders
hotel mementos
decals
hiking trail maps
posters

travel schedule
pressed flowers
drawings
bumper stickers
brochures
ticket stubs
napkins
hotel receipts

Make a pocket page for a road map that shows your route (highlight it). Use duplicate maps to cut out words for your page. Include the names, addresses and photographs of people you meet on your journey. Write down the car games you played; like the License Plate Game or the Alphabet Game. Send postcards to friends. Then, write their names and the message in your scrapbook.

With a car trip scrapbook to keep you focused, you'll double the vacation fun!

BIRTHDAY BASH BOOK

God made you special. What a reason to celebrate! And celebrate you have! From the time you were tiny, your family has trumpeted your birthday with cake, balloons and song. If you're like most kids, -there are photos of you sitting in your high chair, chocolate cake smeared from ear to ear. Or you're in a silly party hat trying to pin the tail on the donkey.

Why not start the book with a picture of you as a newborn? You may want to include a copy of your birth certificate and your just-born height and weight. Then jump to your first birthday party. Include the party invitation, a list of the guests and stuff like that. Work your way up to the present.

Search for snapshots of birthdays with friends at the pizza parlor, or birthday sleepovers with cousins or best pals. How about that birthday at grandma and grandpa's when grandma made you that special cake. And don't forget the picture of all your friends surrounding you opening gifts!

Birthdays are some of your most special times to remember!

Happy birthday to you,

Happy birthday to you,

Happy birthday dear Jason,

Happy birthday to you!

My 10th Birthday

I celebrated with my cousins at Cross Lake, Mn.

The whole gang

Me and my Bud - Joel

Ten candles to blow out!

Happy Birthday

Putting together a whistle-blowing birthday album is a happy way to celebrate who you are, and always remember all those happy, happy birthdays!

COUSINS
BY THE DOZENS

Cousins can be wonderful, irreplaceable, special friends that just happen to be your relatives! They share a lot in your history and holiday get-togethers. Whether you have dozens of cousins, or just a few special ones, you may want to start a cousin scrapbook. Pull photos out of all the great times you've had together. If your stack of photos gets a foot tall, you'll have to find a way to sort it out.

Why not start your book with a family tree? There are lots of ways to display one. For this project, think about drawing a huge oak tree with spread branches. Crop photos of your family and cousins into leaf shapes and "hang" them on the limbs. All the cousins from one family branch will be on one limb and all of the others on another. Label the pictures with each cousin's name and age. Fill the rest of the pages with photos of the fun you and your cousins have together. Take the time to make this book special. Remember, friends may come and go, but cousins are forever!

GRANDPARENT'S GIFT

They've been handing out hugs since you can remember. They never forget your birthday. They listen to all your stories and share their own. You're lucky, your grandma and grandpa really are GRAND! Show them how much you love them by creating a special grandparent's day album. Or make some special pages for them to include in their own scrapbook.

Begin this project long before you need it completed. It may take a while to find the right photos. Contact your grandma and grandpa and other family members. Ask to borrow their favorite pictures of grandma and grandpa. Explain that you're looking for old photos and new ones. Also, borrow memorabilia like baptism and wedding certificates, diplomas, birth announcements, and newspaper clippings that help tell the story.

Interview your grandparents
in person or by phone...

That means, ask them lots of questions about what they've done during their lives. Find out how they feel about important things that have happened in the world. Ask them about their "favorites;" like ice cream flavor, color, and holiday. (For LOTS more questions use the form on page 112.) You may want to record your conversation or have them fill out the form themselves. It's up to you.

Once you have all the stuff you need to include in the album, it's time to put the book together.

Suggestions

* Begin with a title page that says the name of the book. It could be something like, "Grandparents are Grand!" Make the page extra-special.

* Make a dedication page that says something like, "This book is dedicated to my grandparents, Gordon and Marilyn Haglund, September 1999. I love you!" Decorate the page with pictures of all of you doing something special together.

* Put the oldest photos and memorabilia at the beginning of the book and work your way to the present.

* Sprinkle your grandparents' memories (the answers they gave you to the questions you asked) throughout the book. It's great if their answers go with photos! Include memories that other family members have about your grandparents; ask them to send you handwritten notes to share and include as memorabilia.

I love you! That's why I want to know more about you. Can you help me learn by filling out this form? Thank you so much!

YOUR FULL NAME

Date and Place of Birth:

Full Names of Sisters and Brothers:

Full Names of Parents:

GRANDPARENTS

What did your grandparents do?

How did they meet?

What were they like?

What did they like to do for fun?

What made them laugh?

What made them angry?

Did you get to spend much time with them?

What did their house look like?

What's your favorite memory about your grandparents?

PARENTS

What did your parents do?
Where did you and your parents live when you were growing up?
What was it like?
What was the best time of the year in your home?
What was your least favorite chore?
Tell me about your siblings.
Tell me about a time that you got in trouble.
What was the most wonderful thing that happened in your childhood?

FAVORITES

What was your favorite:
Book, Movie (as a child and adult),
Expression, Car, Place, Song,
Class, Sport, Color, Food, Fun?

HOPES, DREAMS & REFLECTIONS

If you could do anything at all, what would you want to do the most?
What do you want me to learn that you consider of great value for me to know?

All aboard! Next stop, Vacation Station where you'll find great ideas for putting together a one-of-a-kind vacation scrapbook.

ADVENTUROUS VACATIONS

Whether you travel by train, bus, car, or plane, you're sure to end up in a "don't-wanna-forget-this" location. And, just as surely, you'll have tons of snapshots to remember it by. Now's the time to make sure those photos of you having the time of your life don't end up in some box in a closet. It's time to start an adventurous vacation album!

When you put together your book, remember to include memorabilia like ticket stubs, postcards, maps, and programs. Journal about the best and worst things that happened. The worst things will make the best stories later. If you're a plan-ahead type ,decide to set aside time to write about your experiences each evening before you collapse in exhaustion. When putting together the book, try to re-create the mood of the vacation spot with color and design. Make this book as happy as those days you spent on your vacation.

CAMP AND CAMPING FUN

It's about fishing and hiking and bonfire sing-alongs. It's about telling scary stories in the dark tent with only one flashlight (and your brother has it). Whether it's family camping, or a kids-only camp; you're sure to have great photos that bring back the smell of that crisp country air. Now's the time to pull your photos together on special camping pages you can enjoy while waiting for your next outing.

Camping pages are great when they're wrapped in a nature theme. Surround your photos with die cuts and stickers of trees, flowers, fish, and animals. Give your pages a bit of "punch" with cloud, sun, and tree punch art. Photo copy the leaves and flowers you collected on your camping trip or do "leaf printing" directly on your page using an acid-free ink pad and a brayer (a "mini-rolling pin", available in craft stores). Cut out images from your campsite brochure and use them to decorate your album pages. Why not make a color photo copy of your trail map and use that to mat photos?

Don't forget to include journaling in your book. Write out the lyrics to camp songs, "how-to" instructions on camp projects (like weaving friendship bracelets); drawings and information about animals or plants; and the names, addresses, and photographs of camp friends. Add to your camp album each year and before you know it, you'll have a pack full of memories to enjoy further down life's trail.

Hot DOGS are the best part of camping. Next, comes marshmallows. Just remember not to get sticky stuff in your fur! And talking about remembering... don't forget that taking photos of campfire activities can be tricky. Use your flash after dark.

Congratulations!

You're now a scrapbook graduate! This trophy is for you, but the real trophies are the albums you're going to create.

HAPPY SCRAPBOOKING!

WRAPPING IT UP

You've done it! You are now a certified scrapbooking whiz. You know how to crop and mat. You know how to use a die cut, punch, or rubber stamp to turn a ho-hum page into something great! You know all about the wild and wonderful tools available to help you make the most of your scrapbooking hours. And, you know much, much more!

Finishing this book is not an ending— it's a BEGINNING! You can now look forward to all those wonderful years of picture taking, page designing, and album creating. The scrapbooks that you begin today will be treasures you share with your children tomorrow. Fifty years from now you'll find yourself sitting with your grandchildren on your lap, turning the pages of the scrapbooks you designed when you were their ages. Because you use safe products in creating your album, those papers and photos will be as clean and clear as they were the day you placed them in your book.

So, pick up your album and dream up an image of an unforgettable memory. Snatch up your scissors and photos, and begin to turn that memory into a reality. You'll find yourself growing more confident and competent with each page you create. Your book will be a reflection of your love of scrapbooking. Your book will be a reflection of the times in which you lived. Your book will be a reflection of the unique person you are!

SURVEY

We're interested in you. Fill out and return this survey. Mail to: TweetyJill Publications, Inc., 5824 Bee Ridge Road, Suite 412, Sarasota, Florida 34233. Your comments mean even better books for you, write to us.

Name ....

Address ....

City .... State .... Zip ....

Age (optional) ....

Did you buy this book? ....

If not, who bought it for you? ....

What are your favorite things to take photos of? ....

....

....

What are your other hobbies? ....

Are you currently working on a scrapbook or have you finished one? Tell us about it, please. ....

....

How would you rate what you learned in this book

A LITTLE	SO-SO	GOOD STUFF	LOVED IT	LEARNED A TON (WANT MORE)